ANIMAL OPPOSITES

Prickly and Soft ANIMALS

Mark Carwardine

Wayland

Titles in this series

Noisy and Quiet Animals

Daytime and Night-time Animals

Quick and Slow Animals

Big and Small Animals

Sleepy and Busy Animals

Warm-Weather and Cold-Weather Animals

Dull and Colourful Animals

First published in 1988 by

Wayland (Publishers) Ltd.
61 Western Road, Hove
East Sussex BN3 1JD
England

British Library Cataloguing in Publication Data

Carwardine, Mark
    Prickly and Soft animals.—
    (Animal opposites)
    1. Animals—Juvenile literature
    I. Title   II. Series
    591   QL49

ISBN 1–85210–414–7

Created and produced by
Ilex Publishers Ltd
29–31 George Street
Oxford OX1 2AJ

Illustrations by Martin Camm, Dick Twinney
and John Francis
Courtesy of Bernard Thornton Artists

Typesetting by Optima Typographic, London
Printed in Spain by Gráficas Estella, S.A.

Cover illustration by Jim Channell
a porcupine and a panda

Contents

Porcupine   4
Bushbaby   6
Spiny Anteater   8
Chinchilla   10
Stickleback   12
Llama   14
Hedgehog   16
Panda   18
Tenrec   20
Rabbit   22
Index   24
Glossary   24

Some words in this book are printed in **bold**; you can find out what they mean in the glossary on page 24.

The porcupine is a prickly animal.

It uses its coat of needle-sharp **quills** to frighten off bobcats, hyenas and other enemies.
This porcupine is eating a leaf.

Porcupines are related to guinea-pigs. There are many different kinds, living in North and South America, Europe, Africa and Asia.
Some are able to climb trees, others prefer to shuffle along the ground.

The bushbaby is a soft animal.

Its fur is thick and woolly and it has a long, bushy tail.
This young bushbaby is following its mother around while she searches for food.

Bushbabies have big eyes, for seeing in the dark. Their ears are large, too, and they can hear even the slightest sound. They feed on tree **gum**, insects, lizards, mice and small birds.

The spiny anteater is a prickly animal.

It looks like a giant hedgehog with a long nose.
This spiny anteater is licking up a swarm of ants with its long, worm-like tongue.

Spiny anteaters, or echidnas, as they are sometimes called, are very unusual **mammals** because they lay eggs.
Most mammals do not. They live in the mountains, forests, plains and valleys of Australia and New Guinea.

The chinchilla is a soft animal.

Its thick, silky coat helps to keep out freezing cold winds.
This chinchilla is nibbling at a leaf with its long front teeth.

Chinchillas live high up in the barren and rugged mountains of the South American Andes. Their front teeth never stop growing, so they often gnaw on hard substances to wear them down.

The stickleback is a prickly animal.

It has three spines along its back.
This brightly coloured **male** stickleback is trying to attract a **female**.

In spring the male stickleback's throat and belly turn a bright red and his eyes turn bright blue. He dances to a female to invite her in to his nest, which lies on the bed of a river, pond, lake or **estuary**.

The llama is a soft animal.

It looks like a woolly camel with no hump.
This llama has a baby which is only a few
days old.

Llamas are closely related to camels.
They have been tamed by the peoples of the
Andes Mountains of South America and are
often used to carry loads.

The hedgehog is a prickly animal.

It has about 5,000 sharp spines all over its back.
This hedgehog has curled up into a tight, prickly ball because there is a dangerous animal nearby.

The first hedgehogs probably appeared over fifteen million years ago. There are now about a dozen different kinds around the world, including five kinds of hairy hedgehogs, which live in south-east Asia and do not have any spines.

The giant panda is a soft animal.

It is one of the **rarest** animals in the world, famous for its beautiful thick black-and-white coat.
This giant panda is eating a piece of bamboo.

Giant pandas live only in a few remote mountain areas of China. Their main food is bamboo, which they munch for hours at a time, sometimes eating as much as nine or ten kilograms every day.

The tenrec is a prickly animal.

Some of its spines are orange in colour, a few are white and the others are black. This tenrec is sniffing the ground for insects or earthworms to eat.

There are over twenty different kinds of tenrecs, most of which are found only in Madagascar. Although some of them look rather similar to hedgehogs, others look more like shrews or moles.

The rabbit is a soft animal.

It has beautiful silky brown fur and a fluffy tail.
This rabbit is sitting in a field and sniffing the air.

The European rabbit is one of the most familiar of all the world's forty-four different kinds of rabbits and hares. Outside Europe, it is also found in north-west Africa, Australia, New Zealand, the USA and South America.

Index

Africa 4, 22
Andes Mountains 10, 14
Anteater 8
Asia 4
Australia 8, 22
Bushbabies 6
China 18
Chinchilla 10
Estuaries 12
Europe 4
Hedgehog 16
Lakes 12
Llama 14
Madagascar 20
Mountains 8, 10, 18
New Guinea 8
New Zealand 22
North America 4
Panda 18
Ponds 12
Porcupine 4
Rabbit 22
Rivers 12
South America 4, 10, 14, 22
Stickleback 12
Tenrec 20
USA 22

Glossary

Estuary The part of a river where it joins the sea.
Female An animal that is, or can be, a mother.
A woman is a female human being.
Gum A sticky liquid from plants and trees.
Mammal A warm-blooded animal, usually with fur.
Female mammals feed their young with milk which they
produce themselves.
Male An animal that is, or can be, a father.
A man is a male human being.
Quills The sharp, stiff hairs on a porcupine.
Rarest Rare means uncommon or not often found.
The world's rarest animals are the least common and
most difficult to find.